CINCINNATI

NL WEST

REDS

MICHAEL E. GOODMAN

Published by Creative Education, Inc.
123 S. Broad Street, Mankato, Minnesota 56001

Art Director, Rita Marshall
Cover and title page design by Virginia Evans
Cover and title page illustration by Rob Day
Type set by FinalCopy Electronic Publishing
Book design by Rita Marshall

Photos by Allsport, Tom Dipace, Duomo,
Focus on Sports, National Baseball Library,
Bruce Schwartzman, The Sporting News,
Sports Illustrated, UPI/Bettmann and
Wide World Photos

Library of Congress Cataloging-in-Publication Data

Goodman, Michael E.

Cincinnati Reds / by Michael E. Goodman.

p. cm.

Summary: A team history of the 1990 World Series
champions.

ISBN 0-88682-462-1

1. Cincinnati Reds (Baseball team)—History—
Juvenile Literature. [1. Cincinnati Reds (Baseball
team)—History.   2. Baseball—History.]   I. Title.
GV875.C65G66 1991   91-10382
796.357'64'0977178—dc20   CIP

THE HOME OF THE REDS

Cincinnati, Ohio, is one of the smallest major league baseball cities, yet it has been responsible for lots of baseball firsts. Cincinnati is the home of the world's first and oldest pro baseball club. The Cincinnati Red Stockings fielded their first team in 1869, just a few years after the Civil War. The Cincinnati team was also a charter member of the National League when it was formed in 1876.

In addition, Cincinnati was the site of the first night baseball game, in 1935. The first and only pitcher to throw back-to-back no-hitters—Johnny Vander Meer— pitched for the Reds. And Pete Rose, the player who is first in major league history in hits, games, and times at bat, not only played most of his career for the Reds but was also born in Cincinnati.

Cincinnati-born Pete Rose.

Cincinnati is traditionally baseball's "opening day city." Most years, the first game of the season is played there. Opening day tickets are sold out every year, usually by Christmas. When the long-awaited opener finally arrives, the conservative citizens of Cincinnati have a wild celebration. A huge parade wanders through the bustling city streets. Offices and stores close early. Students with tickets are allowed to miss class to join the thousands of cheering fans at Riverfront Stadium, the home of the Reds.

The opening day crowd hopes to see the Reds start another great season, one that might result in a National League pennant or even a world championship. The fans wish that today's Reds might follow in the footsteps of the very first Cincinnati team, which didn't lose a single game in its first season!

THE FIRST "WRIGHT BROTHERS" FLY HIGH

The original Cincinnati Red Stockings were formed in 1869 by a Kentucky jeweler and cricket player named Harry Wright. The team's best player was Harry's brother George. These Wright Brothers started professional baseball more than thirty years before another pair of Wrights invented the airplane.

The Wrights recruited the best players in the country to play on their team by offering to pay them. Players' wages started at eight hundred dollars per year. The Red Stockings traveled around the country playing any team that wanted to challenge them. They got lots of challenges in that first year, but not a single loss. The team won by incredible scores such as 80–5 and 103–8.

One of today's best, infielder Chris Sabo.

1 9 0 5

Cy Seymour won the Reds' first batting championship, hitting .377, a Cincinnati record that still stands.

The winning streak had reached 130 games, before a team from Brooklyn, New York, edged the Red Stockings in eleven innings, 8–7. The Red Stockings claimed that they lost the game because a Brooklyn fan jumped on a Cincinnati outfielder while he was fielding a ball. Still, the loss stood.

Harry Wright was the team's manager. He was also a pretty good player, who once smacked seven home runs in a single game. But George Wright was the real star. He was an outstanding fielder at shortstop and a remarkable batter. During that first season in 1869, he batted .629, hit forty-nine homers, and scored 339 runs—in the first fifty-seven games!

The Red Stockings were not only good, they were also tough. After his playing days were over, George Wright attended a baseball game. He came away from the contest sneering, "Imagine, players wearing gloves. We didn't need them in our day."

THE TAINTED WORLD CHAMPIONSHIP

By the turn of the century, the once proud Reds (the name was shortened in the 1880s) had fallen on hard times. Between 1900 and 1916, the team never finished above fifth place in the National League. The club's fortunes began to turn around in 1916, when future Hall-of-Famer Christy Mathewson was brought in as player-manager. Mathewson pitched only one game for the Reds and managed for just two seasons, but he started things moving in the right direction.

In 1919, everything came together for Cincinnati. Pitchers Slim Sallee, Hod Eller, and Dutch Ruether won fifty-nine games among them. Outfielder Edd Roush, a future Hall-of-Famer, won his second batting title with a .321 average, and third baseman Heinie Groh wasn't far behind at .310. The Reds ran away from their National League competition and finished the season nine games in front of the New York Giants. They were set to play in their first World Series ever against the best team in baseball, the Chicago White Sox.

Yet something strange happened. Even though the White Sox should have been favored, oddsmakers began giving the edge to Cincinnati. It was suspected that several White Sox players had been bribed to lose on purpose so that gamblers could make a lot of money.

Edd Roush said after the series, "Compared with the White Sox, we were just an ordinary team. We had no World Series experience, while they had beaten the Giants in the 1917 series with practically the same team. Yet the odds switched so drastically that before the first game, the Reds had become favorites.

"Naturally, I didn't believe anything was wrong then, and I refused to believe everything wasn't on the up-and-up even after we won the first two games. But I must admit things were happening on the field, day after day, that seemed peculiar, to say the least. I just didn't want to—couldn't—believe that anything was wrong."

But something clearly was wrong. White Sox pitchers threw wildly for one or two innings a game, and Sox fielders botched routine plays. With this extra help, the Reds won the best-of-nine series, five games to three.

A year later, the fix was brought out in the open, and eight Chicago White Sox players were banned from baseball for life for throwing the World Series.

1 9 1 9

Under new manager Patrick Moran the Reds finished their finest season with 96 victories.

"Tom Terrific" — *Tom Seaver.*

Outfielder Eric Davis.   11

The real victims of the "Black Sox Scandal" were the Cincinnati Reds. To this day, no one has ever given them credit for winning the World Series. No one believes they were really baseball champions in 1919. One Reds player later remarked, "One thing that's always overlooked in the whole mess is that we could have beat them no matter what the circumstances. We were a great team." Unfortunately, no one will ever know if the Reds could have won that World Series fair and square.

LOMBARDI LEADS REDS TO THE TOP

It would be twenty years before the Reds returned to the World Series. The year was 1939, and the team's leader was one of the best hitters—and slowest runners—of all time, catcher Ernie Lombardi.

12

Two things distinguished Ernie Lombardi: his hitting ability and his big nose, which earned him the nickname "Schnoz." Schnoz batted over .300 in his first year with Cincinnati, and kept his average above .300 in nearly every one of his seventeen major league seasons. This was a pretty remarkable statistic because Lombardi was such a slow runner. He could never beat out an infield hit and sometimes had trouble getting to first on shots to the outfield. "In Cincinnati, once," he recalled with a laugh, "I hit the left field wall and they threw me out at first." What Lombardi failed to mention, however, was just how hard he had hit that ball to allow the fielder to make the play.

Ernie Lombardi was one of seven Reds named to the NL All-Star team.

Despite his slowness afoot, Lombardi is one of only two catchers in baseball history to win a batting crown—and he did it twice. He led the National League in batting in 1938 with a .342 average and was named the league's Most Valuable Player. He also won a second batting title in 1943. Eventually he was elected to baseball's Hall of Fame.

Lombardi was best known as a hitter, and consequently he never received all the praise he deserved as a catcher. He helped to develop the best pitching staff in the National League in the late 1930s and early 1940s. When Johnny Vander Meer established an amazing record in 1938 by throwing back-to-back no-hitters, Lombardi was the catcher in both games. That wasn't an easy chore. "Vandy was real hard to catch because he was so wild," Lombardi said. "You never knew where the ball was going to end up when he was pitching."

Lombardi also helped to make big winners of pitchers Bucky Walters and Paul Derringer. Walters and

Joe Nuxhall became the youngest major league player in history when he pitched aginst the Cardinals at age 15.

Derringer had a combined record of 94—40 in 1939 and 1940, when the Reds won consecutive National League titles and one world championship. Modestly, Lombardi never took credit for the pitchers' fine showings. "You could sit in a rocking chair and catch those guys. Their control was so good," he said.

In 1939 the Reds were favored to win the National League pennant, and they did. Lombardi and first baseman Frank McCormick were the hitting stars, while pitchers Walters and Derringer won twenty-seven and twenty-five games, respectively. The Reds were no match for the New York Yankees in the World Series, however. The Yanks won in four straight, holding the Reds to just eight total runs.

Lombardi and the rest of the Reds were better prepared in 1940. The team repeated as National League champs, and then roared past the Detroit Tigers in seven games for Cincinnati's second world championship—and this one wasn't tainted!

ROBBY AND THE REDS REVIVAL

Ernie Lombardi's birthplace—Oakland, California—was also the hometown of the next great Reds star, Frank Robinson. Robinson arrived in Cincinnati in 1956, as the Reds were building the most powerful batting order in the National League. The team already had three sluggers: muscleman Ted Kluzewski at first base and outfielders Wally Post and Gus Bell. The twenty-year-old Robinson could match those veterans in power, but he was a better hitter for average a better and run scorer than the others.

14   *The hard-throwing Norm Charlton.*

*Besides Robinson,
Ted Kluszewski
(right) also added
strength to the Reds'
lineup, belting 35
homers.*

Robinson was also a daring batter and fielder, who would sacrifice his body to win. At bat, he refused to allow pitchers an edge. "Pitchers like to have the whole plate to work with—to come in on you and go away from you. I decided to give them the inside part of the plate and protect the outside corner by standing as close as I could to home," he said. That meant that Robinson's head was often right over the plate in what was known as "concussion alley." Pitchers often threw in close to him, forcing Robinson to move back or hit the ground. But if the pitcher made even a slight mistake, Robinson made him pay with a scorching line drive or a soaring homer.

In the outfield, Robinson was just as reckless, crashing into walls to make catches. In the first few months of his rookie season in 1956, Robinson crashed into a wall and was stunned or knocked out completely six

Current Reds' star, Randy Myers.

Like Robinson, Chris Sabo was an aggressive player.

For the second time in three years slugger Frank Robinson (right) hit over 30 home runs.

times. Each time, he got up slowly with the help of his manager or teammates and kept on playing. Finally, manager Birdie Tebbetts said, "Look, Frank, the next time you hit a wall, I'm not going to leave the dugout. I'm getting too old to walk 450 feet for nothing."

In 1956, Robinson provided Tebbetts and Reds fans with the best all-around play that Cincinnati had seen in many years. He batted .290, scored a league-leading 122 runs, smacked thirty-eight homers, and drove in eighty-three runs. He was the unanimous choice as National League Rookie of the Year. He had an equally fine year in 1957, and was ready for an even better one in 1958 when near-disaster struck.

During an exhibition game in April 1958, Robinson was hit in the head by a high inside pitch. He lay unconscious on the ground. His closest friend on the team, Vada Pinson, said, "I tried to walk out and see him, but my legs wouldn't take me. I thought he was dead." Luckily, Robinson recovered completely, though he was afraid to crowd the plate for several months.

Despite Robinson's heroics, the Reds just couldn't reach the top of the National League—until 1961. Before that season several writers referred to the Reds as "ragamuffins" and predicted that they would finish in sixth place. But Robinson batted more than .300 in April and May and better than .400 in July to push the Reds into first place. Vada Pinson joined him in the Reds "hit parade" that year with a .343 average, and Gene Freese slammed twenty-seven homers. The pitching stars were Joey Jay and Bob Purkey. Robinson brought the season to a climax with a late-inning pennant-clinching home run on September 26. The Reds had won their first National League crown in twenty-one years.

1 9 6 3

With 204 hits, Vada Pinson led the NL in that category for the second time in three years.

Injuries and money battles with the Reds management caused Robinson to think about retiring in the early 1960s. Gene Mauch, manager of the Philadelphia Phillies, said, "I know ninety-one pitchers in the league and nine managers who will chip in five hundred dollars apiece if Robinson will go through with his plans to retire. That's fifty thousand dollars!"

Instead, the Reds traded away their star after the 1965 season, thinking he was washed up. They regretted that move the next season, when Robinson led the American League in batting, home runs, and runs batted in ("Triple Crown") and was named the American League's Most Valuable Player. He is still the only player in history to win the MVP award in each league.

Hall of Famer Johnny Bench.

"LITTLE JOE" OILS THE "BIG RED MACHINE"

Reds fans were sad to see Robinson leave in 1965, but they didn't grieve very long. A group of new stars began arriving in Cincinnati in the mid-1960s to take his place. Together they formed one of the greatest dynasties in National League history—the "Big Red Machine."

The Reds didn't have to look far to find the first gear of their machine. He was a hometown boy named Pete Rose. Rose was strong, tough, and versatile. During his days with the Reds, he was an All-Star second baseman, third baseman, and outfielder. A great student of baseball history, Rose played with the intensity of old-time great Ty Cobb, whose hitting records he would eventually break. His aggressive play earned him the nickname "Charley Hustle."

Rose specialized in getting on base so he could be driven in by Johnny Bench and Tony Perez. Bench, from tiny Binger, Oklahoma, was to become the finest defensive catcher in National League history and a superb power hitter. Bench's peers recognized his greatness right away. In his rookie year, Bench played in the All-Star game. At that game, baseball legend Ted Williams handed Bench an autographed ball, on which he had written: "To Johnny Bench, a sure Hall-of-Famer." Williams's prediction turned out to be accurate.

Perez, a native of Cuba, was "Mr. Consistency." He drove in ninety or more runs for nine straight seasons with the Reds. His powerful hitting and solid fielding, as both a third baseman and first baseman, helped Cincinnati reach the World Series four times during the 1970s.

1 9 7 0

On June 30, Riverfront Stadium opened to a crowd of over 50,000 cheering fans.

23

Left to right: Joe Morgan, Tony Perez, Johnny Bench, Don Gullett.

The final, and perhaps most important, component of the Big Red Machine arrived in Cincinnati in 1972 via a trade with the Houston Astros. That player was Joe Morgan. Most baseball players can do one or two things well—hit for average, hit for power, run the bases swiftly, or field a position skillfully. Joe Morgan could do all of these things. He was one of the game's most complete players. His greatness was recognized in 1990 when he was elected to the Hall of Fame.

Sparky Anderson, at age 36, led the Reds to the NL pennant in his first season as manager.

Morgan brought not only his skills but also his confidence with him to Cincinnati. "To be a star," he once said, "you've got to have a certain air of arrogance about you, a cockiness, a swagger on the field that says, 'I can do this and you can't stop me.' It's always been part of my makeup. Maybe it comes from being a little guy."

"Little Joe" was only 5'7" and 155 pounds, but he played like a much bigger man. He inspired his teammates to play "above" themselves, too. Morgan used his speed and aggressiveness on the bases to drive opposing pitchers crazy and give Cincinnati batters an edge. "If the pitcher is concerned about you on base, he isn't concentrating enough on the batter. You're doing something without doing anything. You're out there making a difference," he said.

With Morgan, Rose, Bench, and Perez, the Reds became the top team in the National League during the 1970s. They won twelve championships during the decade—six Western Division titles, four National League pennants, and back-to-back world championships in 1975 and 1976.

Perhaps Morgan's and the Big Red Machine's finest hour came in 1975 in the World Series against the Boston

Ken Griffey of the Big Red Machine (pages 26–27).

On September 11, Pete Rose recorded his 4,192 hit, breaking Ty Cobb's all-time major league record.

Red Sox. The Sox made a miracle comeback in game six of the series to force a seventh game. Then Boston jumped ahead 3–0 in the finale, but the Reds clawed their way back to tie the game going into the ninth inning.

Reds outfielder Ken Griffey led off with a walk. He was sacrificed to second base and then advanced to third on the second out of the inning. Pete Rose walked, and Little Joe strode to the plate to face Boston relief pitcher Jim Burton. Burton got two quick strikes on Morgan and was going for the strikeout.

"I was looking for something down the middle that I could drive for a hit," Morgan said. "But the ball was a hard slider, low and away—a perfect pitcher's pitch. All I could do was try to get the bat on the ball, and I hit that darn blooper."

The blooper did the trick. It dropped in front of fast-charging Boston centerfielder Fred Lynn, allowing the winning run to score. Cincinnati had captured its first world championship in thirty-five years.

DAVIS POWERS THE 1990S REDS

The Reds duplicated their World Series triumph in 1976, sweeping the Yankees in four games. Cincinnati thus became the first National League team to win consecutive titles in more than fifty years. However, the Big Red Machine soon began to age and come apart, as key players like Rose, Morgan, and Perez left for new clubs while other stars retired. The Reds slowly dropped from the top of the standings.

Starting in the mid-1980s, the club began a rebuilding process that is beginning to show results. The central

*For his fine perfor-
mance in the World
Series Jose Rijo (left)
was named series
MVP.*

figure of the "new" Reds is a tall, thin slugger from Los
Angeles named Eric Davis—the closest thing to a
complete player since Joe Morgan.

Davis knows that Reds management and fans count on
him to lead the club on both offense and defense. He
once commented, "I'm supposed to steal bases. I'm
supposed to hit home runs. I've run into walls. I've
jumped over walls to make catches." The only problem
is that Davis's aggressiveness has sometimes caused
him to miss games because of injuries. "I could play
more games each year," he said, "but I would have to
change my style."

Luckily, Davis isn't expected to do everything on his
own. Other key players for the new Reds include third
baseman Chris Sabo, National League Rookie of the Year
in 1988, and shortstop Barry Larkin, a double threat

Reliever Rob Dibble.

Shortstop Barry Larkin.

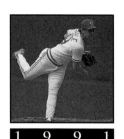

Rob Dibble was the Reds' aggressive leader as they defended their World Series title.

in the field and at the plate. Lefty Tom Browning (one of the few pitchers ever to toss a perfect game) and righties Jose Rijo and Jack Armstrong head Cincinnati's starting pitching staff.

The Reds also have put together the league's most devastating—and crazy—bullpen. The three key relievers, Norm Charlton, Rob Dibble, and Randy Myers, have earned the nickname "Nasty Boys" because of their wicked pitches and outlandish behavior. One teammate said, "They should really be called 'The Looney Tunes.'"

As the 1990 season began, former Yankee great Lou Piniella was named Reds manager. Piniella, who was known for all-out competitiveness when he was a player, brought that attitude to the Reds players, too. Under their new manager, the club tied a major league record by winning their first thirteen games in 1990. Cincinnati never fell out of first place for one day in 1990, as the club roared to its first National League West title since 1976. Then the Reds dismantled the Pittsburgh Pirates in the National League play-offs to earn the right to face the defending champion Oakland A's in the World Series.

Most experts said the 1990 World Series would be a short one, possibly a four-game sweep. The experts were right—except for one thing. They expected the A's to sweep the Reds. Instead, Cincinnati dominated the series, winning four straight contests. "We beat them fair and square," said Chris Sabo. "We're number one now!"

The Reds expect to stay on top for many years to come. Today's Reds aren't a "machine" yet. It will take several more championships for them to be able to make that claim. But the club is beginning to hum. And that has Cincinnati fans singing a happy tune.